T H E *beauty and inspiration of music must not be restricted to a privileged few but made available to every man, woman and child. That is why great music associated with motion pictures is so important, because motion pictures reach millions all over our country and all over the world. Their influence is immensely powerful and deep. We cannot measure how greatly music and motion pictures contribute toward a higher standard and enjoyment of living, increasing the well-being of each one of us, as well as our nation, by giving us not only recreation and pleasure, but stimulation and nourishment of the mind and spirit.*

D EEMS TAYLOR, through his role of music critic, composer, author and radio commentator, has played an essential part in making fine music vitally interesting to millions of people.   When Walt Disney and Leopold Stokowski first discussed F A N T A S I A, they immediately agreed that Deems Taylor should be called upon to aid in the selection of the program as Taylor understands so well America's musical likes and dislikes.   Thus he became not only an important factor in the selection of the eight numbers which comprise the score of the production, but makes his feature motion picture debut by appearing on the screen between selections, commenting on the music in his well-known manner.

WALT DISNEY'S

FANTASIA

in

TECHNICOLOR

and

FANTASOUND

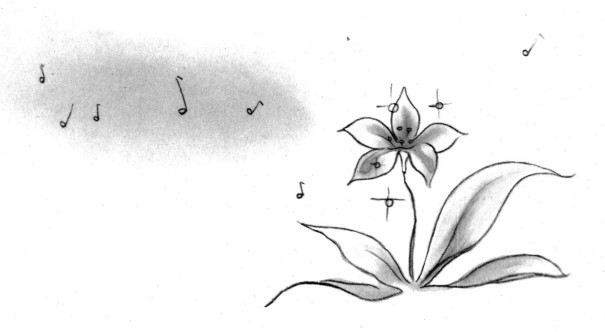

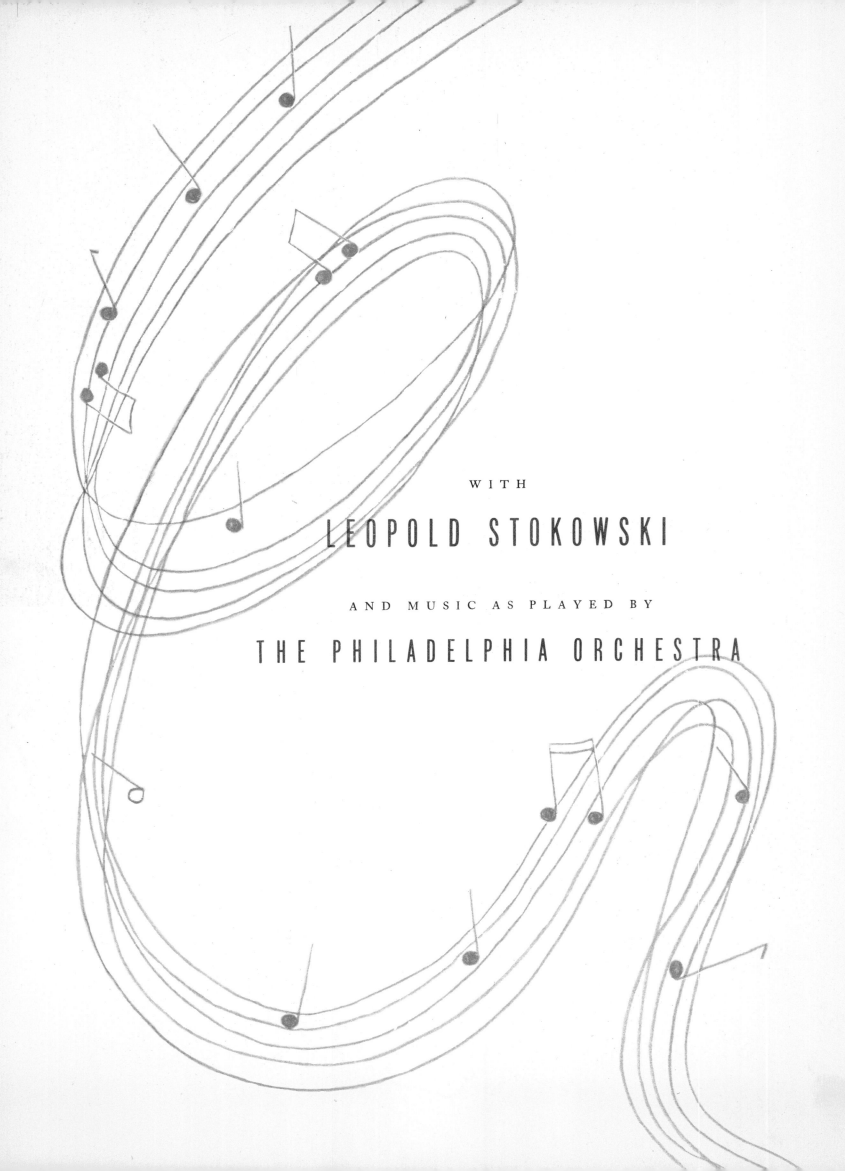

WITH

LEOPOLD STOKOWSKI

AND MUSIC AS PLAYED BY

THE PHILADELPHIA ORCHESTRA

PRODUCTION SUPERVISION	BEN SHARPSTEEN
STORY DIRECTION	JOE GRANT DICK HUEMER
MUSICAL DIRECTION	EDWARD H. PLUMB
MUSICAL FILM EDITOR	STEPHEN CSILLAG
RECORDING	WILLIAM E. GARITY C. O. SLYFIELD
	J. N. A. HAWKINS

FANTASOUND

Recorded by RCA *and reproduced*
by specially designed RCA FANTASOUND *theatre equipment*
developed in collaboration with the
WALT DISNEY STUDIO

Photographed in

MULTIPLANE TECHNICOLOR

Approved

Certificate No. 5920

PROGRAM

TOCCATA AND FUGUE IN D MINOR
Johann Sebastian Bach

THE NUTCRACKER SUITE
Piotr Ilich Tchaikovsky

THE SORCERER'S APPRENTICE
Paul Dukas

RITE OF SPRING
Igor Stravinsky

INTERMISSION

THE PASTORAL SYMPHONY
Ludwig van Beethoven

DANCE OF THE HOURS
Amilcare Ponchielli

NIGHT ON BALD MOUNTAIN
Modeste Moussorgsky

AVE MARIA
Franz Schubert

NOTE: *From time to time the order and selection of compositions*
on this program may be changed.

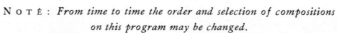

IN *a profession that has been an unending voyage of discovery in the realms of color, sound and motion,* FANTASIA *represents our most exciting adventure. At last, we have found a way to use in our medium the great music of all times and the flood of new ideas which it inspires. Perhaps Bach and Beethoven are strange bedfellows for Mickey Mouse, but it's all been a lot of fun, and I want to thank Leopold Stokowski, Deems Taylor and all my co-workers for holding my head up when the water got too deep.*

FANTASIA

AN ARTIST'S ADVENTURE IN MUSIC

Walt Disney is not a musician. The majority of his artists aren't musicians either. They, like most of us, are just good listeners. Faced with the tremendous problem of translating the music of FANTASIA into pictures, they simply listened and tried to capture the moods, movements, situations, colors and characters which the music painted on the canvas of their imaginations. The results are so inspiring that hereafter the average listener should be much less humble about his ability to understand good music.

But making FANTASIA was a far more complex undertaking than just listening and painting what happened to flash into the imagination. The host of impressions had to be organized and expressed in harmony with the rhythm and structure of the music itself. The herculean nature of the task becomes evident as you see that the artists have not only remained faithful to the spirit of the various compositions, but they have also, for the most part, translated the very phrases and measures and even individual notes into just the right colors and actions. The perfection of color blending, color harmony and color meaning in FANTASIA is remarkable.

It was natural that Walt Disney turned to Leopold Stokowski and Deems Taylor for guidance in the building of FANTASIA and its recording by the great Philadelphia Orchestra. Both men have been active leaders in bringing a wider understanding of good music to the general public. Both are deeply interested in the experiments to improve the quality of sound reproduction. It should be of great importance to the general public and to the entire motion picture industry that Disney technicians, in collaboration with RCA, have designed a revolutionary system of sound reproduction, christened "FANTASOUND," which gives a directional and third dimensional effect. In FANTASIA, the audience hears the music of a great symphony orchestra with a new, rich realism that is startling.

In the past, composers have been able to turn only to the comparatively limited mediums of opera and ballet for an interpretation of their works in color and motion. Stokowski, Taylor and Disney believe that FANTASIA will suggest to the great composers of our day, a third medium — a medium where color and motion are restricted only by the limits of imagination — the medium which is giving to the public FANTASIA, that new kind of entertainment which has been described as "seeing music and hearing pictures."

TOCCATA AND FUGUE

DIRECTION . . . . Samuel Armstrong

STORY DEVELOPMENT . Lee Blair
Elmer Plummer
Phil Dike

ART DIRECTION . . . Robert Cormack

BACKGROUND PAINTINGS Joe Stahley
John Hench
Nino Carbe

ANIMATION . . . . Cy Young
Art Palmer
Daniel MacManus
George Rowley
Edwin Aardal
Joshua Meador
Cornett Wood

It is quite natural to think of music in terms of visual colors. We frequently speak of a "blue" note, while more than one hundred years ago, the great Beethoven was exhorting the men of his orchestra to give him "more purple" in certain passages, "more gold" in others. And later Rimsky-Korsakov executed color scales and Scriabin composed Promethe for colored lights (first performed by Leopold Stokowski and the Philadelphia Orchestra). There followed an experimental concert in which Stokowski combined the music of the Philadelphia Orchestra with a color organ.

Walt Disney and Stokowski wished to make the overture to FANTASIA a further experiment in interpreting the colors and moving patterns of music in colors and moving patterns on the screen. The *Toccata and Fugue* was chosen not only because it is magnificent music but also because it lends itself to this type of interpretation — it being music which neither seeks to tell a story nor paint a picture, but exists solely for the beauty of its own tone patterns.

Although Bach (1685-1750) had been dead for many years before the other composers represented in FANTASIA were born, it is revealing to learn that distinguished critics of our day often say that his music is still "more modern than the moderns."

DIRECTION	SAMUEL ARMSTRONG
STORY DEVELOPMENT .	SYLVIA MOBERLY-HOLLAND
	NORMAN WRIGHT
	ALBERT HEATH
	BIANCA MAJOLIE
	GRAHAM HEID
CHARACTER DESIGNS .	JOHN WALBRIDGE
	ELMER PLUMMER
	ETHEL KULSAR
ART DIRECTION . . .	ROBERT CORMACK
	AL ZINNEN
	CURTISS D. PERKINS
	ARTHUR BYRAM
	BRUCE BUSHMAN
BACKGROUND PAINTINGS	JOHN HENCH
	ETHEL KULSAR
	NINO CARBE
ANIMATION	ART BABBITT
	LES CLARK
	DON LUSK
	CY YOUNG
	ROBERT STOKES

THE NUTCRACKER SUITE

Tchaikovsky

DANCE OF THE SUGAR PLUM FAIRY   *The Dewdrop Fairies*

CHINESE DANCE . . . . *Hop Low and the Mushroom Dancers*

DANCE OF THE REED FLUTES . . *Blossom Ballet*

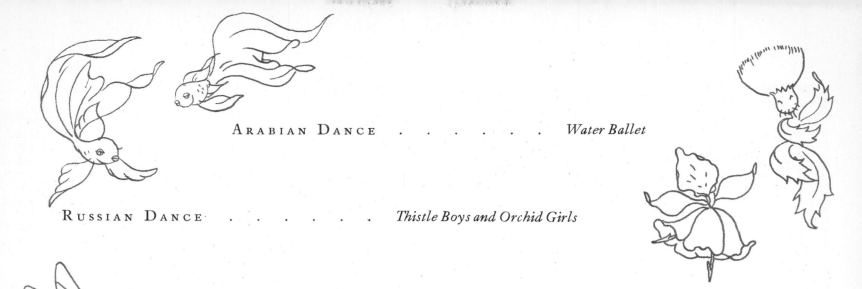

ARABIAN DANCE . . . . *Water Ballet*

RUSSIAN DANCE . . . . *Thistle Boys and Orchid Girls*

WALTZ OF THE FLOWERS . . . . *Autumn Fairies, Milkweed Ballet,*
Frost Fairies, Snowflake Fairies

THE MUSIC of the *Nutcracker Suite* takes you to a realm of purest fantasy where the things you've dreamed about become reality. You won't see the little girl and the handsome nutcraker-prince of the old tale around which the music was written, for they're in the audience, having their glimpse of this enchanted fairyland with you.

With a master of imagination as your guide, you'll discover why the flowers and grasses sparkle in the sunshine . . . what goes on beneath the surface of a quiet stream . . . what makes the leaves change colors . . . what snowflakes really are . . . and that a clump of thistles or a cluster of mushrooms may not be just what they seem.

This triumph of beauty has also been a triumph of technical skill. When Disney started work on FANTASIA, many of the problems presented by the *Nutcracker Suite* were not only unsolved, they were unheard of. No one at that time knew how to light a scene with incandescent dewdrops or how to animate the intricate geometrical patterns of a host of dancing snowflakes. But when the artists demanded such effects, the Disney technicians achieved them.

They devised new ways of handling paints and pastels. They explored new methods of manipulating the giant multiplane camera, new developments in lighting, unusual process shots and many spectacular tricks that go under the general heading of "special effects." In short, the artists conceived the impossible and then the technicians made it not only possible but practical, until finally the fairyland of their imagination was captured and brought to you in FANTASIA.

Fantasia in the making

9

4

5

6

7

8

1 As soon as the music for FANTASIA was selected, Disney artists started the delicate task of transferring the mood and story of each composition to the animation medium. Here, Sam Armstrong, one of the picture's eight directors, explains the progress of his sequence to Walt Disney, Stokowski and Taylor.

2 Each minute of the completed picture represents weeks of hard work. Out of "sweatbox" sessions (staff meetings) come new angles, criticism, and spirited exchanges of ideas. FANTASIA'S production supervisor, Ben Sharpsteen, meets with four of his sequence directors: Paul *(Rite of Spring)* Satterfield, Wilfred *(Night on Bald Mountain-Ave Maria)* Jackson, Jim *(Sorcerer's Apprentice)* Algar, and Bill *(Rite of Spring)* Roberts.

3 Norm Ferguson, co-director on *"Dance of the Hours,"* shows Deems Taylor some choreographic patterns for the Ostrich ballet.

4 Although Disney legend has it that artists grow to look like the characters they create, animator Bill Tytla, responsible for the fiendish devil character in *"Night on Bald Mountain,"* stoutly maintains that any resemblance is purely co-incidental.

5 For the first time on the Disney lot, "live action" crews photographed human characters for certain sequences in FANTASIA. First to go before the Disney camera was Leopold Stokowski. Hollywood musicians were the source of orchestra shadows.

6 The greater part of FANTASIA was made in Disney's new studio in Burbank, California. Disney has built a streamlined, air-conditioned home for his personnel of over 1,000 men and women.

7 Acetate records were made of each of the FANTASIA compositions to aid artists in their pictorial interpretations. Dick Huemer and Joe Grant, the picture's story supervisors, and Deems Taylor listen to a recording of Beethoven's *Pastoral Symphony.*

8 When Taylor and Stokowski first checked in at the studio, they spent hours with Walt Disney listening to his colorful version of the new type of picture on which they were to work. Preliminary story sketches helped Disney put his points across.

9 The obviously anonymous artist who drew this sketch of the Boss titled it "I don't like it!" Walt Disney's facial expression is one that his staff frequently sees when he confronts something that is good, but not good enough.

THE SORCERER'S APPRENTICE

Dukas

I T   A L L started about twenty centuries ago when a Greek writer named Lucian made up a story about a powerful magician and his little assistant. A thousand years later, the German poet, Goethe, liked the story and wrote a poem about it. A hundred years or so after that, Dukas, a Frenchman, turned the poem into music. And now, an American named Disney has put the whole thing into the movies!

Walt Disney has been experimenting with the idea of turning music into pictures since his first Silly Symphony, *The Skeleton Dance*, released in 1929. The tale of the Sorcerer's Apprentice had always amused him and obviously only his unique medium could realize the full humor of its situations.

DIRECTION . . . . . . JAMES ALGAR

STORY DEVELOPMENT . PERC PEARCE
                             CARL FALLBERG

ART DIRECTION . . . TOM CODRICK
                             CHARLES PHILIPPI
                             ZACK SCHWARTZ

BACKGROUND PAINTINGS CLAUDE COATES
                             STAN SPOHN
                             ALBERT DEMPSTER
                             ERIC HANSEN

ANIMATION SUPERVISION FRED MOORE
                             VLADIMIR TYTLA

ANIMATION . . . . . . LES CLARK
                             RILEY THOMPSON
                             MARVIN WOODWARD
                             PRESTON BLAIR
                             EDWARD LOVE
                             UGO D'ORSI
                             GEORGE ROWLEY
                             CORNETT WOOD

So, with an orchestra of players individually chosen from the finest instrumentalists in Los Angeles, and with Leopold Stokowski conducting, the Dukas music was recorded and Walt Disney's artists started to work. The role of the apprentice was a natural for Mickey Mouse. The studio staff became fascinated by the possibilities which this new venture opened up. When the preliminary sketches and test reels had been made, Disney called in everyone he could lay his hands on in order to get a typical audience reaction. The carpenters and gardeners were invited, the traffic boys and the girls from the Inking department, visiting celebrities and the woman who ran the hamburger stand across the street. Everyone was enthusiastic, and the encouraging thing was that these people were not trained musicians. They didn't know any more about classical music than the Disney artists themselves.

That is how FANTASIA began, and just as the magic in the story went far beyond the little apprentice's original intention, so did the idea of making great music visual grow into the revolutionary kind of entertainment that is FANTASIA.

1

FANTASOUND is a revolutionary achievement in sound reproduction. Its development by R C A and the Disney Studio was a natural outgrowth of a desire to bring to motion picture audiences the dynamic range and true tone color of the symphony orchestra . . . freed from the mechanical limitations of ordinary methods of recording and reproducing.

In FANTASIA, you will be able to experience the orchestra's full richness of tone and subtlety of phrasing just as though you were hearing an actual concert in the Philadelphia Academy of Music or in Carnegie Hall.

The performance of the Philadelphia Orchestra, under Stokowski, was simultaneously recorded by nine sound cameras. One camera concentrated on the overall blend and the other eight obtained "close-ups" of the individual instrumental choirs. By the separation of the orchestral components, fullest advantage may be taken of the dramatic possibility of the musical compositions.

"Fantasound" points the way toward new developments in the future of entertainment and its use in FANTASIA is only the beginning.

1 Leopold Stokowski watches while Bill Garity, Disney's chief engineer, synchronizes the recording of FANTASIA sound tracks. Intensely interested in the improvement of music recording and reproduction, Stokowski believes that the new *Fantasound* will revolutionize the presentation of music in motion pictures.

2 Not only must an expert music cutter be able to "read" a complete orchestral score, but he must know how to find corresponding notes on a film sound track. Stephen Csillag, Disney's musical film editor, uses a Moviola to locate a bassoon note for one of FANTASIA's sequences.

3 In recording the music for FANTASIA, the Philadelphia Orchestra was divided into eight instrumental choirs. The music was then recorded through nine channels and thirty-three separate microphones. Deems Taylor and Ed Plumb, musical director, examine one of the nine sound track projectors which were used in the re-recording of the music.

2

3

RECORDING IN PHILADELPHIA

1 Leopold Stokowski in rehearsal. In Philadelphia's Academy of Music, he leads the members of the Philadelphia Orchestra through the complex score of FANTASIA. The candid camera does much to capture the dramatic force so widely associated with Stokowski.

2 Walt Disney and some of the studio staff made a special trip to Philadelphia for the recording of FANTASIA music. Walt and musical director Ed Plumb talk over the next day's recording plans with Stokowski, just before an evening performance of the Philadelphia Orchestra.

3 On the stage of the Academy of Music, Stokowski conducts the forceful music of Stravinsky's *"Rite of Spring."* Only in rehearsals does he use a score . . . in concert, never.

4 Musical beats for an animated picture must be strictly timed before Disney artists take up the task of drawing. Walt inspects the tempo-recording machine as some of the music is played back.

5 The intricacies of recording call for a little relaxation now and then. During the momentary absence of the harp player, Walt Disney tries his hand on this instrument, while Deems Taylor confuses him with the mystery of the glissando.

RITE OF SPRING

DIRECTION	BILL ROBERTS
	PAUL SATTERFIELD
STORY DEVELOPMENT &	
RESEARCH	WILLIAM MARTIN
	LEO THIELE
	ROBERT STERNER
	JOHN FRASER-MCLEISH
ART DIRECTION . . .	MCLAREN STEWART
	DICK KELSEY
	JOHN HUBLEY
BACKGROUND PAINTINGS	ED STARR
	BRICE MACK
	EDWARD LEVITT
ANIMATION SUPERVISION	WOLFGANG REITHERMAN
	JOSHUA MEADOR
ANIMATION	PHILIP DUNCAN
	JOHN MCMANUS
	PAUL BUSCH
	ART PALMER
	DON TOBIN
	EDWIN AARDAL
	PAUL B. KOSSOFF
SPECIAL CAMERA	
EFFECTS	GAIL PAPINEAU
	LEONARD PICKLEY

THE RITE OF SPRING has been called modern music's Declaration of Independence. Yet, its premiere in Paris was never finished. The audience hooted, whistled and yelled until the curtain had to be rung down. The explosive impacts of discordant sound, its raw violence, its brutal, pounding rhythms were too much for the outraged audience. That was in 1913. Today, the music is better understood, and many musicians, including Stokowski, consider it one of the greatest and most significant compositions of all time.

As originally staged, *The Rite of Spring* represented primitive life in a series of tribal dances and rituals. But Disney and his artists heard in this awesome music the vast pageant of the primitive, and so, in impressionistic sweeps through time and space, this visualization tells a story of the first two billion years upon our planet. Music less violent and shocking than Stravinsky's would be inadequate to express what is unfolded in FANTASIA—convulsions of a new-born world, cataclysmic upheavals that remoulded the face of the earth, and the death battles of incredible monsters who several hundred million years ago roamed over what is now Paris, New York, Hollywood . . . and our own backyards.

In picturing a primitive world, Disney has let Science write the scenario. Such world-famous authorities as Roy Chapman Andrews, Julian Huxley, Barnum Brown and Edwin P. Hubbell volunteered helpful data and became enthusiastic followers of the picture's progress.

Scientists tell us that the fifty-ton monsters and flying dragons and sea-serpents you will see are creatures which once actually lived and looked as they appear on the screen. But while scientific authorities have been able to reconstruct the skeletons of the long-extinct dinosaurs so that we have an accurate picture of their size

Igor Stravinsky, the only contemporary composer represented in FANTASIA, has long been an admirer of Walt Disney's work. When the *"Rite of Spring"* was chosen, the composer watched its interpretation with keen interest.

and shape and weight, it was not until FANTASIA that anyone had seen such monsters live and breathe and move and die. And only after long months of study of skeletal remains, of balance and weight, were the Disney artists able to conclude how these creatures must have moved. Stegosaurus and pterodactyl became as familiar to them as their own pets. Eustocenopteron became plain old Eustace, and all the strange creatures of *The Rite of Spring*, from the one-celled microscopic organisms to the giant killer Tyrannosaurus Rex, were as living personalities to the studio staff.

The combination of Stravinsky's stark music with Disney's dramatic portrayal of the primitive carries such a terrific impact that it was decided to place *The Rite of Spring* just before the intermission so that audiences might have time to recover from the tension of its violent mood.

1

5

2

3

4

1 On the set at the Disney studio, Deems Taylor steps from the Technicolor shadows of his feature film debut for a sandwich-and-coffee snack.

2 To Bambi and Faline, the live models for Walt's forthcoming feature B A M B I, Stokowski, Taylor and Disney were not three famous personalities, but rather a trio of affable gentlemen who came calling almost daily.

3 Deems Taylor "adjusts" his makeup before facing the camera for his part in F A N T A S I A. This shot should steady, somewhat, those confused people who have heard Taylor say: "Well, I'm in F A N T A S I A and yet I'm not."

4 Robert Benchley, frequent studio visitor, seems to be weighing the ballet as a possible theme for a future dissertation entitled "How to Enjoy the Ballet or Should I Give Up Starches?"

5 Deems Taylor as he looked to a Disney caricaturist who was slightly under the influence of Beethoven's Pastoral Symphony.

THE PASTORAL SYMPHONY
Beethoven

DIRECTION	HAMILTON LUSKE	
	JIM HANDLEY	
	FORD BEEBE	
STORY DEVELOPMENT .	OTTO ENGLANDER	
	WEBB SMITH	
	ERDMAN PENNER	
	JOSEPH SABO	
	BILL PEED	
	GEORGE STALLINGS	
CHARACTER DESIGNS .	JAMES BODRERO	
	JOHN P. MILLER	
	LORNA S. SODERSTROM	
ART DIRECTION . . .	HUGH HENNESY	
	KENNETH ANDERSON	
	J. GORDON LEGG	
	HERBERT RYMAN	
	YALE GRACEY	
	LANCE NOLLEY	
BACKGROUND PAINTINGS	CLAUDE COATES	
	RAY HUFFINE	
	W. RICHARD ANTHONY	
	ARTHUR RILEY	
	GERALD NEVIUS	
	ROY FORKUM	

ANIMATION SUPERVISION FRED MOORE
WARD KIMBALL
ERIC LARSEN
ART BABBITT
OLIVER M. JOHNSTON, JR.
DON TOWSLEY

ANIMATION . . . . BERNY WOLF
JACK CAMPBELL
JACK BRADBURY
JAMES MOORE
MILT NEIL
BILL JUSTICE
JOHN ELLIOTTE
WALT KELLY
DON LUSK
LYNN KARP
MURRAY McCLELLAN
ROBERT W. YOUNGQUIST
HARRY HAMSEL

An obscure German composer named Justin Knecht wrote a second-rate composition called *A Musical Portrait of Nature*. When nature-loving Beethoven heard Knecht's work he declared loudly that Nature had been libeled. To rectify this grievous slander, Beethoven took Knecht's theme, the beauties of the country, and built on it his famed *Pastoral Symphony*, giving it the sub-title *Recollections of Country Life*.

Writing of the *Pastoral Symphony*, Beethoven said, "It is *feeling* rather than tone-painting . . . I leave it to the listener to discover the situations for himself . . . Anyone with a notion of country life will imagine the composer's intentions."

Walt Disney has taken Beethoven at his word. He has imagined the situations for himself. But with a fine disregard for the obvious, Disney's imagination has leaped nine thousand feet upward to the summit of Mount Olympus and thousands of years backward into mythology, remaining faithful, however, to the *Pastoral* spirit.

The music itself, of course, is performed just as Beethoven wrote it. But where Beethoven pictures a quiet brook in his native countryside, Disney pictures a brook where the winged horse, Pegasus, and his family swim together. And when the music mirrors a happy gathering in the country, Disney shows not villagers and peasants but rather fauns and cupids, centaurs and centaurettes frolicking in a harvest festival in honor of Bacchus, tipsy god of wine. When Beethoven calls for a storm, Disney gives you a storm, but it is a storm made by Zeus and Vulcan leaning from the clouds and tossing giant thunderbolts to earth. And, as the music tells of the calm after the storm, Disney tells of Iris, goddess of the rainbow, and Apollo, whose chariot is the sun . . . of Diana, who shoots her star-tipped arrow from the crescent moon . . . of Morpheus, with his all-enveloping cloak of night, who brings sleep to the tired world.

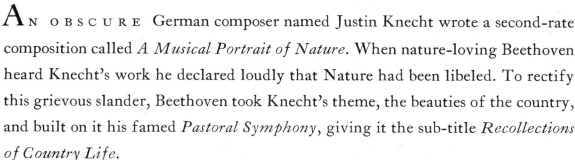

1

2

6

3

4

5

WELL-KNOWN VISITORS PREVIEW FANTASIA

1 Kirsten Flagstad, one of the world's truly great singers, was thrilled with the musical interpretations worked out by Disney and his staff. Walt Disney shows Madame Flagstad one of the character models for FANTASIA.

2 Actress Katharine Cornell is introduced to some FANTASIA "actors" by director T. Hee, artist James Bodrero, and director Hamilton Luske.

3 Choreographer George Balanchine delightedly shows Igor Stravinsky one of the ballet dancer models from *"Dance of the Hours."* A leading ballet figure of the country, Balanchine declared that the Disney treatment of the dance reached a new high in technique.

4 Walt Disney shows Dr. Edwin Hubbell of the Mt. Wilson Observatory and Dr. Julian Huxley, the biologist, a model of Triceratops, one of the characters in *"Rite of Spring."* Scientists who visited the studio appreciated the efforts toward prehistoric authenticity in the Stravinsky sequence.

5 During a trip to Hollywood, members of the much-discussed Association of American Artists visited the studio in a body. George Biddle, association director Reeves Lewenthal, Thomas Hart Benton, Ernest Fiene, Grant Wood, and Georges Schreiber have a field day with models for FANTASIA characters.

6 Igor Stravinsky as sketched by a Disney caricaturist. Stravinsky was delighted . . . and now possesses the original.

DANCE OF THE HOURS

Ponchielli

DIRECTION	T. HEE
	NORM FERGUSON
CHARACTER DESIGNS .	MARTIN PROVENSEN
	JAMES BODRERO
	DUKE RUSSELL
	EARL HURD
ART DIRECTION . . .	KENDALL O'CONNOR
	HAROLD DOUGHTY
	ERNEST NORDLI
BACKGROUND PAINTINGS	ALBERT DEMPSTER
	CHARLES CONNER
ANIMATION SUPERVISION	NORM FERGUSON
ANIMATION	JOHN LOUNSBERY
	HOWARD SWIFT
	PRESTON BLAIR
	HUGH FRASER
	HARVEY TOOMBS
	NORMAN TATE
	HICKS LOKEY
	ART ELLIOTT
	GRANT SIMMONS
	RAY PATTERSON
	FRANKLIN GRUNDEEN

ALTHOUGH Ponchielli's *Dance of The Hours* was first performed at La Scala, Milan, in 1876, it remains today a glorious example of the *danse classique* at the pinnacle of its full fruition. The ballet occurs in the third act of the opera La Gioconda (The Smiling One) as the Duke Alvise entertains his guests with a divertissement in the grand ballroom of the palace. The distinctive choreography, so charmingly baroque, yet at the same time so daringly conventional, is permeated with the true spirit of the early idiom and presents a significant commentary on the eternal struggle between the powers of light and darkness.

As the curtain rises, Mlle. Upanova, *solo ballerina*, symbolizes the dawn as she summons her dancers, the early hours, to her side in a series of graceful *arabesques*. The ballet chorus, in classic patterns, *sur les pointes*, follows her about the spacious hall until, in a lovely tableau, they kneel at the edge of a sunken pool. Then, as a nymph arising from the waves, Hyacinth Hippo emerges from the pool. Her hand-maidens circle about her in the vivacious *faux pas*, executed from the second position, portraying with tender nuances the languor of the day.

Now, to the music's *mode minor*, a new *corps de ballet* interprets the twilight hours, and although there is still a gay abandon in the superb *pirouettes* of Elephanchine, there is a hint of something to come, a half-veiled, illusive mood of breathless desire. And it comes! Ben Ali Gator, *maitre de ballet*, sweeps in with his sinister band, heralding the sullen approach of the hours of the night. In a magnificent *cherchez la femme*, the chorus leaps about in bold *double entendres*, while their leader executes the brilliant *triple entente* with virile grace.

The music's quickened tempo foretells the return of Hyacinth Hippo. She is timorous before Ben Ali Gator as he, entranced with her beauty, makes a *passe-partout* in her direction. Then, suddenly infatuated, she surrenders to him in the electric measures of the *adagio* as he lifts her triumphantly above his head in a swift *demi-nelson*. In the grand finale, the *tout ensemble* expresses the transcience of night and the victory of day in a spirited *allons a buffalo*.

When we see what this talented troupe does to *l'arte des danse* in the true classic tradition, we can only marvel at what the future may hold.

NIGHT ON BALD MOUNTAIN AND

Moussorgsky

No MUSIC approaches *Night on Bald Mountain* in the feel of sheer, elemental terror. It reeks with Death; it howls, shrieks and thunders Evil. It could have been conceived only in the imagination of a genius like Moussorgsky. Once, as he listened to *Bald Mountain*, Moussorgsky cried out to the gods of pagan Russia for the power to see the demons and monsters which he heard racing through this music.

DIRECTION . . . . WILFRED JACKSON

STORY DEVELOPMENT . CAMPBELL GRANT
ARTHUR HEINEMANN
PHIL DIKE

ART DIRECTION . . . KAY NIELSEN
TERRELL STAPP
CHARLES PAYZANT
THOR PUTNAM

BACKGROUND PAINTINGS MERLE COX
RAY LOCKREM
ROBERT STORMS
W. RICHARD ANTHONY

ANIMATION SUPERVISION VLADIMIR TYTLA

ANIMATION . . . . . . JOHN McMANUS
WILLIAM N. SHULL
ROBERT W. CARLSON, JR.
LESTER NOVROS
DON PATTERSON

SPECIAL ANIMATION
EFFECTS . . . . . . JOSHUA MEADOR
MILES E. PIKE
JOHN F. REED
DANIEL MACMANUS

SPECIAL CAMERA
EFFECTS . . . . . . GAIL PAPINEAU
LEONARD PICKLEY

AVE MARIA CHORUS: Charles Henderson, *Director*
Julietta Novis, *Soloist*

AVE MARIA

Bald Mountain is near Kiev in Southern Russia. In pagan times, according to tradition, the worshippers of Evil gathered on its wind-swept summit to do homage to Tchernobog, the Black God. One of these demoniac revels which Moussorgsky's music describes has been re-created by Disney's artists.

Just as Moussorgsky was a pathetic child of Darkness, the genial, guileless, lovable Schubert was a child of the sun. The two compositions associated in FANTASIA are reflections of their violently contrasting personalities. This very dramatic contrast undoubtedly appealed to Disney, the dramatist: *Bald Mountain*, the epitome of universal Despair and Evil; the *Ave Maria*, a universal symbol of Hope and Good; the fundamental conflict between Good and Evil, Life and Death.

Then, too, it was felt that the sacred beauty of the *Ave Maria* would provide an emotional relief to audiences tense from the shock of Moussorgsky's malignant music and its grim visualization.

In a universal language, music, the *Ave Maria* sings of peace and hope and life. Schubert himself said it was written as an act of spontaneous devotion springing from an overpowering emotion.

Crossing the natural bridge of music from *Bald Mountain* to *Ave Maria*, far away in the dim light of first dawn is seen a band of hooded pilgrims carrying torches. They move through avenues of tall-trunked trees. As the light increases, the trees take on natural gothic forms until the forest seems to have become the interior of a cathedral, immense, stately and beautiful beyond the dreams of human architects.

Disney's treatment of *Bald Mountain* and the *Ave Maria* will be recognized by creative people as surpassing in technique, imagination, power and freedom of conception, anything which the animator's art so far has brought to the public. In thirteen superb minutes, one sees the new horizon of animated pictures, a great art which can be at the same time pure entertainment.

It should be noted that the lyrics sung in F A N T A S I A's version of the *Ave Maria* are not those from Sir Walter Scott's "*Lady of the Lake*," which Schubert used, but were written for the picture by the distinguished American novelist and poet, Rachel Field.